My Best Friend

By
John D. Cook

With thoughts and memories from family and friends

To my loving wife and best friend, Linda,

I love you!!!

Let the words of my mouth, and the meditation of my heart,
Be acceptable in thy sight, O Lord,
My strength, and my redeemer.

Psalm 19:14

"For My thoughts are not your thoughts,
Nor are your ways My ways", says the Lord.
For as the heavens are higher than the earth,
"So are My ways higher than your ways,
And My thoughts than your thoughts."

Isaiah 55:8 - 9

Acknowledgements

Without the continual encouragement and unfailing love of my family and friends, this book would have been just a continuous, nagging, and probably a passing thought but certainly not a reality. I thank the good Lord above, for planting the seed of desire within me, to write this, the will to persevere through its completion, and the wisdom to put my thoughts (and those thoughts and memories of others) into words.

A deep sincere "thank you" to Jeremy and Randi, Christopher and Ixcheal, Ashley and Zachary, Marion and Clay, Dennis, Lee and Gloria, Pat, Mary and Patrick, Danny and Stephanie, Ron and Carol, Don and Lorraine, Patty and Harry, Dan and Sharon, Carter and Gay, Larry and Mary Anne, Rick and Gloria, Ron and Anne, Linda B., and Patsy.

Over the years, several people I have had the pleasure to either work or associate with, that have, impressed me with their convictions, morale standards, ethics, leadership, a genuine care for others and a devoted love of family. These individuals have inspired me in numerous ways for which I can never thank them enough: Larry Silvey, Ed Carter, Don Chambers, Jack Avant, John Downey, Ron Willis, Roy Seth, Bob Greathouse, Larry Tennant, Bob Goodin, Rick Bonacci, Dan Berg, and Bobby Wayne, thank you, gentlemen for your inspiration and friendship.

Table of Contents

August 25, 1973

I, John, take you Linda, to be my lawful wedded wife,
To love and to hold,
To honor and cherish,
For richer or poorer,
In sickness and in health,
Till death due us part.

All married couples have repeated vows similar to these over the
years.

Now, before I continue, let me tell you a bit about myself. I am
not a theologian, but I am a Christian. I do not have a doctorate
or a master's degree in divinity or journalism. I spent 22 plus years
in the navy as an aviation storekeeper and an flight crewman. After
retiring from the military in 1991, I did go back to school majoring
in graphic design and illustration. At the start of this writing, I had
been working for a contractor with the NATO Peacekeepers in the
Balkans for the past five and a half years. Basically, just an average
guy, working to support his wife and family, sacrificing time away
from home and his family, in an attempt to provide a better life in
the future.

I met Linda when she was a car-hop at the local A&W Drive-
in, in Oxnard, California where I was assigned to a nearby naval
air station. I had known her for about a year or so, just sort of as
an "older brother" or buddy. She lived around the corner from us,
occasionally stopping by to joke around with us and I would drop her

off at work or into town when she was running late. A relationship slowly started to develop due to similar interests that we had in common. Eventually we started dating and then ultimately, fell in love. We were married on a particularly warm August afternoon and what a beautiful bride she was.

Over the years, she gave birth to our four children, Jeremy, Christopher, Ashley and Zachary. She suffered a miscarriage in the fall of 1977, the day of the Michigan – Ohio State football game. (I remember this because of the interest in the game among the hospital staff and during breaks in the "action", they were quickly checking their patients). She was about five and a half months along in the pregnancy. We tearfully accepted this loss as part of God's plan for us.

So, by now you are probably asking, "Where is this guy going with all this and what exactly is he trying to say?"

"Linda Cook, whose vehicle plunged over the steep side of the road on Libbey Hill April 9, died early April 27 at home in Oak Harbor She was 46. ......"[1]

This is a book about a beautiful Christian woman who was not only my wife, but also my best friend. She was also the mother of our children and "Grandma Cookie" to our grand daughter, Kayla and grandson Parker, who was born a few months after her passing. A woman, who touched the lives of so many with her ever-present smile, an infectious laugh, and a gentle heart of genuine care and concern for others.

And we know that all things work together
for good to those who love God,
to those who are the called according to His purpose.

Romans 8-28

I have often thought about a sermon, I heard not long ago, where the pastor challenged the men in our congregation," to show honor to your wife". A few times in the past, when things didn't exactly go in the direction I was hoping for, she would say, "God has a plan for you, we'll just have to wait and see what He has in mind." Since her death, I believe the Lord has been nudging me in the direction of writing this book and I feel as, not only a tribute to honor Linda, but also what would lead me to the next point.

Since men don't seem to typically purchase a book like this, I must assume that most wives, like my wife Linda, would and then pass it on to the husband in hopes he would read it. I have worked my entire life in the two worst career fields possible, that strains a not only a "healthy" but any marriage – the military and the construction industry. So let me get straight to the point.

MEN, YOU NEED TO FIND THE TIME AND GO THROUGH THIS BOOK WITH YOUR WIFE!!!

Now, I'm not saying our marriage was perfect, but simply, both Linda and I were committed to making it work. (In fact, not long after the wedding, she told me, that the morning just before the wedding, her mother confided in her, that during her bridal shower, several weeks earlier, one individual had made the remark that our forthcoming marriage "wouldn't even last for six months". Well, it not only lasted those six months, but it lasted for a beautiful twenty eight years, eight months and two days.)

Sure, we had our ups and downs, likes and dislikes, and heated discussions as do most marriages, but we didn't throw up our hands and give up on each other like so many we have known over the years. To us, divorce was never even a consideration, let alone a choice or an option. We both strongly believed in the life long commitment of marriage that we had pledged to each other on our wedding day.

I read a book a few years ago, "The Way To A Woman's Heart", and have tried to apply what I learned to our relationship. In one statement Chuck Snyder describes how he and his wife help others through marriage struggles by drawing on their own experiences. He states, *"But rather than trying to get out of the situation, we decided to work our way through them, and now we can pass on to you the same comfort and encouragement God has given us as we have gone through the same situation"*. I see where we and in particular, Linda, have done the same over the years. So, this book is about some of our experiences and experiences and memories of others who have come in contact with Linda.

Linda's Mother's Story

Linda Joyce Lamberson was born August 24, 1955, to Leo and Marion Lamberson in Riverside, CA. She was dedicated to God in October of 1955 and she was baptized September 24, 1964.

"Linda is God's child, He always watched over her." *Marion, August 1, 2002.*

The first five years of Linda's life, she was fortunate to have lived next door to Grandma and Grandpa Lamberson. *(Cora Faye Hiesler Lamberson and Leonard Paul Lamberson)*

Her other grandparents on the Ingram – Edwards *(Thurston Wayne Ingram and Mary Elizabeth Vance Ingram Edwards)* side of the family lived farther away, so she did not know them as well as she knew Grandma and Grandpa Lamberson.

Linda was a happy contented child, she was a goal setter and achiever. She had the ability to laugh at herself. She had love and compassion for others.

She often thanked me for giving her my love, support and guidance.

When she was four months old, I had been Christmas shopping, carrying Linda in one arm and a package in my other. As I was walking to my car and passing the Greyhound bus depot, (a bus was about ready to depart) a crazed, wild eyed gray haired woman came running toward me. She reached for Linda and said, "Give me that baby!" I screamed and quickly turned away from her. I ran into a restaurant and yelled, "Help! Call the police, a woman tried to take my baby". The police made a report, but nothing evolved from this report. The woman hurriedly ran and got on the bus, just as it was departing the depot. To this day, that woman's face is very vivid in my mind.

When Linda was ten months old, Grandpa Lamberson would tease her by putting his feet on the coffee table, and rearranging the crocheted doilies Grandma had put on the arms and backs of the chairs. Linda would shake her finger at him and "jabber" until he properly replaced them.

Linda did not like anything on her head. Her cousin Jim (Hohimer), liked to plop something on her head often, to make her squeal.

She was very fastidious about her shoes. She did not like to have dirt on them. Big brother Dennis, often saw an opportunity to kick dirt on her shoes. She would stomp her feet and say "Dee Dee Wayne (her nickname for him), you stop that.

When Dennis annoyed her, she would say, "Dee Dee Wayne, leave me alone, I do alright".

She was a menace to Dennis when she was three and he was eight. Every evening, we three washed and dried the dishes. This is when Dennis did his spelling lesson. I would say the word and spell it to Dennis and say "sound it out". Before Dennis could complete the word, little sister would complete the word and say "sound it out Dee Dee Wayne". This episode expelled Linda from the kitchen.

She and her dad had special time together then.

She loved to have stories read to her. She learned to read at an early age and was an avid reader throughout her life.

Linda talked a lot, her dad called her "Maggie Magpie". She liked to sing. The first song she learned was "Twinkle, Twinkle Little Star". Her favorite Sunday school song was "Jesus Loves All the Little Children of the World". Her favorite toys were a sock monkey that Grandma Lamberson had made for her, Mary Poppins Doll with accessories and a trunk and Ginny dolls.

Linda loved the outdoor. One morning, Grandpa Lamberson called me on the telephone and said, "look out of your back door, there is a Humming bird on Linda's shoulder". She stood very quietly; it was a Rufous Humming bird. It was a bight copper orange color and shined like a new penny. At no other time or since did we see a Rufous in our area.

She also loved flowers, as she became older, she disliked the chore of helping me pull weeds from the flower gardens. She also loved butterflies. Her dad made a framed collection of various species for her. This has been given to her granddaughter Kayla. She had a great love for animals. Her dad gave her a young lamb but, we had to find a new home for it, as Linda was allergic to the wool.

Her true companion for many years was Cleo, her Beagel dog. She also had Sylvester, a cock-a-poo (a mixture of Cocker Spaniel and poodle) I inherited Sylvester when Linda married John .... Thanks Linda!!!

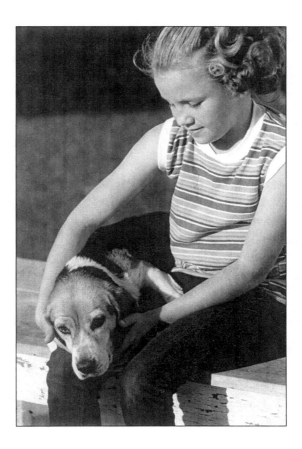

Photo by Leo Lamberson
Linda and Cleo

Among her collection of cats, was "Tiger", a yellow and white striped cat given to her from a friend Mr. Tony. Then along came "Sox", a Himalayan, who happened to follow her home. She carried it to the back gate of the schoolyard, put it down and from there it followed her home.

Linda was working in the office during summer school. The cat came into the room and jumped into Linda's lap. Then from some unknown area came "Fat Cat" … a gray and white striped cat. This too was an inheritance when Linda married.

"Again, God was watching over Linda."

When she was in second grade, she and her classmates and the teacher were on the fenced in playground. A man called to another little girl and said, "What is the name of the little blond curly haired girl who is wearing the blue dress?" The little girl did not answer him but immediately ran to the teacher and told her of the man's inquiry. The teacher took all the children back into the schoolroom. She contacted the school principal, who contacted the police. The little girl gave an accurate description of the car the man got into and left.

Usually Linda walked the two blocks to school with friends but the principal called me to pick up Linda and her friends when school was over. The man was caught one week later at another school.

When we lived in Arlington (near Riverside), Linda's best friend was Judy Kish *(Rita and Ernie Kish's daughter)*, who lived on the street behind us.

When Linda was two and a half years old, everyday she would stand by the front room window and wait for our neighbor Oscar Gerhart, from across the street to come home from work. He would wave to her and say "Hi Linda". Linda would return his greeting with a wave and say, "Hi Oscar". One day she gave her greeting and Oscar did not wave or say hi. Linda came to me and said, "Poor Oscar, he cannot hear anymore".

One spring vacation when Linda was three years old, we went camping in our travel trailer to Red Rock Canyon, in the California Mojave Desert. We became acquainted with another camping family. The dad was a schoolteacher and was observing Linda sitting at the table printing the alphabet. He asked Linda, "How old are you?" She replied, "I am three years old and I am in the first grade". He look astonished and said, "I believe it".

When Linda was almost five years old, the family moved to Port Hueneme, CA. Her dad was manager for U.S. Plywood Co. The office was on the dock and the lumber would come in by barge. These were often unloaded at night. Bob Pallow, a worker from the Los Angeles area would come to help take inventory and unload the barge. After the work was finished about three in the morning, Bob would come home with Linda's dad and sleep until about seven in the morning. We had not lived in the neighborhood long when Linda said to our neighbor, Mrs. Allen, "Do you know Bob Pallow?" Mrs. Allen "No, I don't". Linda said, "he sleeps at our house when Daddy works at night". Mom had some explaining to do to Mrs. Allen.

Linda loved to swing as high as the swing would go. She was told, "Do not jump out of the swing". One time she dared to jump out of the swing as it reached its highest height – results were a broken left arm.

When she was five years old her ambition was to be a school crossing guard so she could "carry the sign".

Linda's favorite teachers were Mrs. Bohn and Mr. Minnick, her fourth and fifth grade teachers, respectively.

When she was in the fifth grade, she met a new friend, Maria. Maria was from Spain. Linda was her English language tutor and Maria taught Linda the Spanish language. When Linda was in the sixth grade we teased her about Alan M.. Alan was a quiet boy and very intelligent. Today, the kids would probably call him a "nerd". He and Linda conversed often, he told her she was the only one who understood him. He asked his mother to buy Linda a Valentine card, but nothing "mushy". Later we would often say, "I wonder what became of Alan M.?"

Linda always had love and compassion for others. When she was twelve, she volunteered to work in a nursing home as a "Candy Striper" (the girls wore pink and white striped aprons)

She liked to help me and one day when I was at work, she washed six new blouses of mine in hot water. They instantly went from a size ten to a size six. I could not reprimand her, all she was doing this to help me.

Linda was elected Princess for Jobs Daughters when she was fifteen and was chosen queen when she was sixteen. Since she liked to sew, she made a royal blue velvet long skirt and a white long sleeved silk blouse for this occasion.

Linda's high school graduation picture

When she was sixteen, we stood side by side and looking down at me she said, "Mom, you sure have low knees". When my 50th birthday arrived, she said, "Gosh mom, you're a half a century old".

Linda always had many friends, she chose to go out in a group, rather than have a steady boy friend. She met John when she was working at the A&W Root Beer Drive In, in Oxnard, California. God blessed her with the true love of her life – John. John is a devoted husband, a loving father and grandfather. Their love for each other and their family strengthened their spiritual growth and continues to be a light for others to follow. Thank you, John, for asking me to share a little bit about Linda's life before she met you.

I have been blessed to have loved Linda from birth, through her childhood and see her become a mature woman of inner and outer beauty, to become a loving devoted wife and loving mother and grandmother.

With Gods' love, trust, wisdom, courage humor, strength and faith, she accomplished every challenge that was presented to her. She believed "to be an inspiration, you had to be inspired". She was an inspiration to all who knew her.

"Linda, you are the light of my life, I love you ….. Mom."

From notes as told by Marion (Lamberson) Stone, 1 August 2002.

Lorraine's Story

Linda, this has taken so long to write, because how do you put into words how much you mean to me.

I lost a sister that April morning. Remember the first time I met you? Wanda invited you to come along with her to my open house for Christmas. Boy, did you act all quiet and reserved. I found out you worked at Chocolates for Breakfast (an espresso shop in town) and you said to come in and have a coffee. I went several times and then was asked to go to a luncheon for Christian Women's Club. Guess who I saw there, up front making everyone laugh … yes, that quiet Linda I had met.

Well, you took me under your wing and soon, I took your place as book chairman. Boy, no one could take your place, but you supported me.

After about a year of getting to know you and your family and couldn't find enough time to spend together.

Your John took a job overseas and all we kept talking about was when you would be quitting your job and then we could spend time together. We started remodeling the inside and outside of your house and loving the time with you, your kids and mine. Well it didn't take long before I took your place at the coffee shop.

I never have had a girl friend I could talk to and share with, like you. You truly are a sister in Christ. Linda, I haven't had a sister like you since. I miss you so much.

Note: Now Lorraine's husband, Don, is a civilian electronics expert working for the navy and I worked for a contractor for the

Army, so we were frequently on assignment overseas. These two women were truly, loving and devoted wives. They would share the pain and trials of separations but they took great delight in making our homecomings unforgettable.

You were so much fun to be with. You could talk me into anything I would have only dreamed of. Remember the time we were at McDonald's and I said I wanted to pickup Don at the airport in only a raincoat? Well by the time we left, I had a raincoat and a dare. We are still laughing about the memory.

Remember going shopping to get some items or the lack of items for your visits with John when he would fly into Canada for his R&Rs?

I miss having someone to talk to about our kids. I never shared with anyone but my honey (Don) about our kids.

Remember this verse:

Trust in the Lord with all your heart,
And lean not on your own understanding;
In all your ways acknowledge him,
And He shall direct your paths.

Proverbs 3: 5 & 6

We used to recite this when we would talk about our kids and all the problems they experienced in life, after all we didn't have the answers all the time.

Do you remember the girl Bud (Lorraine and Don's son) used to go with that we didn't like and you used to let me cry on your shoulder? Then when Dustie (their daughter) worked at Chocolates after school. She also was going out with someone we didn't like, so you would visit the coffee shop in the afternoons, and let us know what was happening. Boy, were we sneaky. But thanks to you, both of our children are married to beautiful Christians.

I remember all the times you always time to listen and help others who were in need, maybe someone who would listen, someone who needed prayers, or someone who just needed help in solving some issue. You always had a kind heart.

We now have grandchildren and I really miss sharing these times with you.

For you were once darkness, but now you are light in the Lord.
Walk as children of light,
the fruit of the Spirit is in all goodness, righteousness and truth,
finding out what is acceptable to the Lord.

Ephesians 5: 8-10

God bless and keep you .... Lorraine

John's Story

L inda worked at an A&W Drive-In, near our house in Port Hueneme, which four of us "sailors" had rented. We found the food to our liking and frequented this fine dining establishment on an almost daily basis. Teen burgers and root-beer, now that was real food!!! Eventually I met Linda through a friend of mine, in the navy. His girl friend happened to be Linda's best friend.

We started dating and eventually fell in love. Our best friends, Linda and AJ, were married about 4 months before we were, and we were both part of their wedding party. It would only be couple of weeks until I proposed to Linda.

Photo by Mary Della Hohimer
Linda and John, on their wedding day in August 1973.

We were married in a Catholic church in Oxnard, but neither of us was what you would call very religious. Sixteen months later, we transferred to an air station in Michigan and started attending Protestant services at the base chapel.

It was while I was stationed there, that our squadron suffered a tragedy: *"A U. S. Navy plane from Selfridge Air National Guard base in Mt. Clemens, crashed and burned as it approached a military airfield ...yesterday, killing all 16 persons aboard.*[2] At one time, I was to have been part of the original crew, but plans and needs of the navy changed and so, I was sent on another detachment to Europe instead. Five days after both of our planes departed the states, "618" crashed. We returned from the detachment early to attend the memorial service. After meeting me at the hangar, waiting for me through a lengthy debriefing, and when she was driving me home, I remember Linda asking me about the crew and my breaking down and crying over the loss of my friends, while she comforted me and she cried too, knowing the hurt I was experiencing. That was the type of person Linda was, always seeking to help or comfort those in need.

The next day at the memorial service, the wife of my friend (and 618's flight engineer), Roy, now a widow, came into the chapel with their five children in trail behind her. Linda would tell me a couple of days later that was the moment she was convinced, "it was time to get right with the Lord again".

So for the next few years, she prayed for my salvation (I guess I'm a little hard headed at times) and in September 1982, I accepted the Lord as my Savior.

Two of the duty stations where I was assigned, it was possible to hear our old planes take off and land, from our house. Over the years, several people have told me that every time she saw or heard my plane take off, she would stop whatever she was doing, say a short prayer and comment, "he's in the Lords' hands now".

As many of you can probably attest to, the life of a military wife is not an easy one and is even harder if the husband is assigned to special units or flight crews where separations, both short and long and are frequently extended, are the norm vice the exception. Some of the duty stations you get assigned to are not your first or second or even last choice. Linda always accepted the transfers to new assignments, looking forward to these with her expression, "new places to explore and people to meet". She always managed to get involved, Sunday school teacher, Scout's mom, youth group mom, 4-H leader, Christian Women's Club and a homeschooler for our four children. No matter how busy she might be, she always had time for someone who was hurting, be it listening to a wife with marital problems, a battered neighbor in need of our couch for a safe night's sleep or helping a teen to solve a major crisis. There had been nights where the two of us would go out and have a young military couple over to baby-sit our kids, just so the couple would have a "good pizza dinner" and a few extra dollars to help them get by till payday.

We were both extremely thankful that the Lord had provided me with a good job. Linda had a very strong servant's heart. I believe Philippians 2:3-4 best describes her spirit;

> *"Let nothing be done through selfish ambition or conceit, but in lowliness of mind let each esteem others better than himself. Let each of you look out not only for his own interests, but also for the interests of others".*

She was always looking to help those who were in need, whether it be a few extra dollars to make a house payment, the admission fee for someone to attend a Promise Keepers event, or even a couple who lost everything in a fire. Every year she would buy books of McDonald's food tickets to hand out to the homeless in Seattle during her and our daughter's annual Christmas shopping trips.

A friend of ours at church needed to certify as a tugboat crewman and their family budget didn't allow that. So Linda sent a check to the church, which in turn took care of getting him taken care of. His wife had it down to two people trying to figure out who had helped. She approached Linda at church, reminding her, she was a Christian and couldn't lie. So Linda admitted, she had sent the check after talking to me, and asked the wife not to tell who had helped. Not wanting praise or thanks, just wanting to help. The wife never told her husband till she spoke at the funeral service.

For the last eight years, from Thanksgiving till just before Christmas, Linda was involved with Chuck Colson's Ministry of Prison Fellowship's, Angel Tree Project, arranging for, collecting, even wrapping and distributing Christmas gifts to children of prison inmates in our area of Washington state.

She was a leader in our daughter's 4-H horse club, and at a recent dedication of a tree and a planter at the fairgrounds in her memory, some comments by other members whom had come in contact with Linda, described her as; "had compassion for newcomers, ... made them feel immediately welcome, ... always so cheerful and willing to help, ... was always so cheerful and she made our club so enjoyable with her sense of humor and bright smile, ... had a fresh view of any stressful situation".

We have tried to instill this same spirit of caring for others, in our children, whether it be painting an elderly woman's fence, cutting another's lawn on a regular basis, or stacking a load of firewood to the surprise of an elderly couple.

The first year I was in Bosnia, I had managed to find a group of army troops and a chaplain who had started an accountability group at one of the camps not far from our base camp. We were using a Promise Keepers study book, but the army chaplain was only provided with two copies of the book for the group, which amounted to twelve of us. I talked to Linda on the phone about it one night after my first meeting with them, and thanks to her, there were books for every one of us within two weeks. Never seeking praise or recognition, just a true spirit of wanting to help.

Linda also had a deep understanding and caring concern for the young married couples she would come in contact with. As a friend and "older sis" to these younger women, she would use our own experiences to help nurture them along. After all, she had been a "navy wife" since she was eighteen and had a wealth of wisdom to pass on. For many of these ladies, it was their first major move to an unfamiliar place (for many, it was their first time away from home) and not knowing a soul.

When Linda taught a young married women's group at our church, she became friends with a very young, pregnant, military wife who had just come up to the island with her young husband. Linda had missed her for a couple of weeks at class, so stopped by to see her. This couple was just getting by as he had less than a year in the military. Linda found her sick and dehydrated and too weak to get out of bed, so she took her to the base hospital for help. The girl was admitted and taken care of. Linda was concerned that the couple's furniture consisted of only an old mattress and two lawn chairs in the apartment. She called a few friends, who in turn called a few more and within hours we had delivered and outfitted their apartment with a couch, chairs coffee table, dining room set, some dishes and pans, a complete bed and dresser.

One of Linda's favorite stories was about our own engagement and wedding, trying to relate that no matter how bad things get, they will get better and in the end you can always have a good laugh about it later. (She was much more animated in telling this than I am.)

I had proposed to her on a Saturday evening, at a family skiing campout at a lake in California. The next day while water skiing, I hit a piece of driftwood and caught the ski in the face, just below my left eye. My older sister, Pat (the nurse) and Linda took me to a local hospital for sutures. A week later I reported to sick call at the base and was admitted to the hospital with Hepatitis (from polluted lake water), which then threatened the already planned wedding date. After two weeks in the hospital I was back at work. California required a blood test before a marriage license could be obtained, which would be questionable up to the last minute because of this illness.

I figured the best way to start out a marriage would be to be debt free, so my only outstanding debt was paid off. And as luck would have it, after renting our apartment, a week before the wedding and while moving our things there, the engine in my van threw a rod, so off to the credit union for a loan to replace it.

The big day arrived, and it turned out to be a hot and sunny California afternoon. In the middle of the ceremony, the maid of honor kneels down and starts to mumble something while the rest of us are standing. When it's time for all of us to kneel she passes out. The priest, looks down at her, didn't miss a beat and while the ushers carried her out, the wedding continued. (A little fresh air and a few minutes sitting in a chair she was fine.)

The second day of the honeymoon, we arrived at Lake Tahoe late in the afternoon, after dinner and seeing the sights we went back to our little chalet. About 1:00 in the morning Linda wakes me up with the side of her face all swollen and in severe pain, we decide to head back home for a trip to her dentist. A few days later he extracted her impacted wisdom tooth. We figured things haven't gone perfect but what else could happen? Well, the next day our photographer calls, or I should say his wife calls and tells us that none of the wedding pictures turned out, because his camera was just out of the shop for repairs and hadn't actually been repaired. Linda sat down and cried over this and started to wonder, "is this marriage going to really work?" After contacting everyone who took pictures at the wedding, we were sent the negatives and we did end up with some great pictures. Things did get better.

She had a great sense of humor and on several occasions performed her "Duct tape" comedy routine. A good family friend, Rick, was always the subject for her demonstration and usually ended up wrapped up in duct tape. Now they had an ongoing 'playful torment' of each other. Linda had always been one to read, and loved to work crossword puzzles, so understandably, she had quite a vocabulary, which wasn't generally known. We were involved in a couples bible study once, where Rick was in charge of the lighter moments and would always have a word game of some sort. She would always do well, which got Rick to thinking, he'll "set her up". So he spent the entire next week searching for the perfect word and presented it to her at the next meeting. She accepted the word and promptly gave the correct answer, which left Rick totally amazed and wondering, "How did she know that, I've never even heard that word before?"

Since Rick, his wife Gloria and daughter Stephanie were in the same 4H horse club as our daughter Ashley, we would camp out together at different horse shows. There were water gun fights and practical jokes. One of Linda's favorite but did backfire on her, was an Oreo cookie (which were Rick's favorite) that she had doctored just for him. After carefully replacing the crème center with toothpaste, she set it out for Rick, but his wife Gloria started to eat it first. Needless to say, this has been brought up numerous times since.

The Journal

"Husbands, love your wives, just as Christ also loved the church and gave Himself for her, that He might sanctify and cleanse her with the washing of water by the word, that He might present her to Himself a glorious church, not having a spot or wrinkle or any such thing, but that she should be holy and without blemish. So husbands ought to love their own wives as their own bodies; he who loves his wife loves himself. For no one ever hated his own flesh, but nourishes and cherishes it, just as the Lord does the church. For we are members of His body, of His flesh and of His bones".

Ephesians 5:25-30

Remember when:

- The first time you met your wife, did you secretly have the thought, "this may be the one"?
- Or how about your first date? Do you remember, what she wore, where you went, and what you did together?
- Your first kiss together? (That was probably like a 4th of July fireworks display)
- How about when you proposed to her? Linda insisted I ask her parents for their permission. (Which is something we have instilled in our children as the proper and respectful thing to do.)

- Your wedding day?
- How about the birth of your children, I was extremely fortunate enough to be there in the delivery room for the birth of each one of ours (this was quite an accomplishment for someone in the Navy, to be home for the birth of all our children). Your child's birth is truly one of God's special miracles.
- How she comforts you in a time of sorrow ..... I had lost several friends in a plane crash.
- Being in the military, we were on many detachments and she was always there to greet me on my return.
- How she is always around to give you that hug, a word of encouragement or just to snuggle up to you when your day wasn't one of the greatest.

Think about how she is always there for you and how you, naturally, assume that she will always be there, I did and then one day you realize she is no longer around. When I came home from the Balkans after resigning my position, to take care of our two youngest children, my oldest son, Jeremy, wanted to pick me up from SeaTac Int'l. Airport and drive me to our home on Whidbey Island. I convinced him it would be easier if I just caught the airport shuttle bus up to the island. The real reason was, I knew how painful it was going to be, to come home knowing this time Linda wouldn't be there to meet me, as had always been the case for the past twenty nine years.

(I've tended to keep a journal over the past few years, that Linda would read, when I'd bring it home on R&Rs. It basically contained what was happening daily since I was assigned to a "hazardous pay area" and just some of my thoughts. So I've included some of the entries. I was going to give this to Linda to read, once she was home and on the road to recovery.)

In my case, I had been home on R&R and had left to return to work in Bosnia on a Thursday. (As many years as we've been doing this, leaving home and saying good-bye, never did get any easier. The trips to the airport were usually quiet, my stomach would always get queezy, just depressed since our time together was always too good but also too short. We had discovered it was easiest, if Linda just drops me at the curb, I give her a hug and a kiss goodbye and I head inside. She would have her cry in the car and head home to the kids while I hide my tears and head to the gate.) The following Tuesday night, I get a call in the middle of the night from the company's Human Resources Office to call home, there's a family emergency.

Journal entries:

4-10-02

After working late again Tuesday night, got back to the room and went to bed. About 1:10 Wed. morning I get a call from the Macedonia H/R Office with the dreaded message "you need to call your family, there's an emergency".

I called the house, no answer. Called both Linda's and Ashley's cell phones, no answer. Called Jeremy, he didn't know of any problems but would check it out. Called Mary, (my sister in California), thinking something has happened to my mom, but no problem there. So I called the house again and talked to Ashley. She said Linda was in an accident and was being flown to Harborview (trauma center in Seattle). Gave me a phone number for Whidbey General Hospital (the hospital on Whidbey Island), 678-7609 and talk to "Jenny". Called and was told about the accident, Linda had a punctured lung, broken ribs, broken ankle and broken face bones, was "packaged" and transported to Harborview. She was alert and talking. Jenny gave me Harborview's number.

In my thinking, Harborview is a trauma center, so there must be more. Called Harborview and talked the ER nurse and the Flight nurse from the helicopter, and they relayed basically the same. Told them I would be there ASAP.

Called the house again and left a message that I was on my way home and they should probably go to Jeremy's. Got with H/R manager, Rich Slater, advised him that I needed to leave immediately. He arranged transportation and an escort from security. Notified my department manager of my situation and was on the way to Zagreb (Croatia) by 2:45 am.

Got to Zagreb at 7:00 am, and checked in at the hotel, the H/R office wouldn't be open till 8:00, so took a shower, called the hospital and talked to the emergency room doctor, who gave me the run down.

- They had to perform surgery to repair a ruptured diaphram, she is on a ventilator, with two chest tubes inserted for drainage, vital signs are good, there should be no problem.
- She has facial fractures, possible broken right wrist, muscle damage to her left leg, broken left ankle, possible multiple broken ribs, numerous minor cuts and abrasions.

Called Jeremy, who is handling things like a pro, what a great kid. He will call Mary to let her know and I called Marion and Lee (Linda's mother and father) to let them know what has happened. H/R made the flight reservations and we left for the airport to catch a 9:05 flight to Amsterdam. Was suppose to leave for Seattle at 2:20pm but the plane had mechanical difficulties and we had repeated delays until the crews time would expire so the flight was cancelled and rescheduled for a Wed. morning. Their backup plane was also broken. We were put up at the airport Hilton. Just called Jeremy for an update. She is heavily sedated, still on a ventilator, but oxygen was reduced from 60% to 40%. Are to do more tests during the day. He did get a hold of Chris and the Red Cross has verified and contacted his Air Force unit. He's been granted emergency leave, will fly out Thursday morning from England. Mary and Pat are flying up Thurs. morning also.

4-11-02 (somewhere over the north Atlantic between Iceland and Greenland)

Didn't sleep much during the night, called Jeremy about 4:30 (Amsterdam time) this morning, she is still heavily sedated but responding to commands to move her toes and fingers. He says she's fidgeting, like she is restless. All the x-rays confirmed no neurological damage and other than the broken bones below her left eye, her head is in good shape and no problems. Possible slight damage to a vertebrae in her lower back. No broken wrist, leg or ribs, although she is severely bruised. She is swelled up considerably. Zach says she's black and blue all over and all cut up from the broken glass. Jeremy signed consent forms to have surgery to repair her ankle (which will required pins and screws), and the muscle and ligament damage Thursday morning. The doctor said they will probably keep her out until this weekend and in ICU till Monday, before they move her to a room.

Jeremy says from the pictures she went up over the guard rail, off the road through some trees before hitting another at the bottom ravine about 80 feet down from the road level. Witnesses said the trailer was fishtailing violently before hitting the guardrail. The trailer looked to have jack-knifed and broke apart from the Bronco ending up, piled along side the truck. About fifteen men were at the scene when rescue people got there and it took over an hour to cut her out of the wreck. Don and Loraine (you couldn't ask for better friends) have collected everything out of the Bronco and trailer, Jeremy has notified Gail Iverson at the insurance company. He says the truck and trailer are both history, they had to cut the keys out of the ignition on the steering column, to get the other keys to the house and van. The glove box is inexcessible. The State Troopers say Linda is lucky to be alive. I like to believe that she had angels watching over her.

Marion will be flying out this afternoon also. Talked to Ashley and Zach who both seem to be doing better than I am, they are both staying at Jeremy and Randi's. The Daltons have made their place available for people to stay when they fly in. Ashley notified her instructors at the college and doesn't have to be there until Monday

We left about 8:30 this morning and are expected to land approx. 9:50, west coast time. The flight crew tried to get me on another flight last night but nothing was available, all flights to the states had already departed. The cockpit crew told me a little while ago, they will get me right off the plane in Seattle and will call ahead to have me rushed through customs. One of the crew has volunteered to run me to Harborview, but I told them Jeremy would be there to pick me up. It's 11:00 now. I just have to sit and wait, which is not the easiest thing to do right now.

Finally arrived in Seattle about 9:30 am. As promised, the flight-crew had arranged for immediate deplaning and ushered through customs (it seemed harder to clear customs leaving the airport than all the times to board the plane). Caught a cab and got to the Hospital about 10:00. Talked briefly to the doctor I had talked to the other night. All of Linda's vitals are real good, she has a slight sinus infection, they say due to the nasal tube, (one of many in her) but they are monitoring that along with everything else. She doesn't look as bad as I was expecting, lots of swelling due to the amount of fluids they introduced to her to fight infections, keep her hydrated, anti-anxiety (for all the tubes inserted) and for pain. Called Jeremy to let him know I was in, he showed up a bit later.

Chris and Marion arrived about 3 – 3:30 with Ashley and Zach. Zach is having a real hard time dealing with this, after all, mom's aren't suppose to be banged up and looking like this. Pastor Ron showed up for a bit. Not much to do except sit, pray and wait, hold her hand and talk to her. She continues responding to commands to wiggle her toes and fingers, grasps and squeezes hands, and nods her head when ask and if she is not in deep sleep. They will advise us on the situations with facial and vertebrae fractures, surgery is questionable in both cases. Pat and Mary have showed up and already, Pat is doing the nurse thing and "questioning the staff", they love that!!!

4-12-02

Spent last night at the house, needed a shower, washed my clothes and tried to relax, just some quiet time to myself. My best friend is not in good shape, hurting and I can't do anything to fix her, except pray, but I know God is watching over her and that is a great relief.

Got up and was about to leave and Patty called and now I know how everyone got notified. Went to the impound yard to look at the Bronco and try to find missing checkbook and cell phone. Only found her old cell phone which is history now. Found one of her hoop earrings which I'd almost swallowed more than once!!!! (Private... Linda knows what I'm talking about). Jeremy has pictures of the car, it's hard to believe she is alive and only hurt like she is, the Bronco looks like no-one could have survived that wreck. <u>God protected her</u>.

Went to the bank and had them freeze the account till we find the checkbook. Called the phone company and had them do the same and send a replacement phone. Stopped by and talked to Loraine and thanked her for all their help.

Back to Jeremy's and then the hospital for the rest of the day. Suppose to operate on her ankle and leg but, one OR is down and emergency case came in also, so postponed till later. Vitals are good still on respirator and drugged into la-la land, she must be in some serious pain but doesn't know it till it wears off a bit, she'll start to squirm and then the nurse boosts her meds and she drifts off.

4-13-02

Bought the kids home last night, Zach did finally go in and hold her hand and talk to her a bit, it's really hard for him.

The kids stayed a home and I headed back down for the day. The kids found the missing checkbook, and went to the crash scene and recovered the cd players, cell phone, groceries (the animals could have those), Ashley's hood and the lic. plate. I'm finding it relaxing to get home and sleep in our bed and get a few things done at night.

I sent out an email daily to keep everyone up to date on her condition.

Here's the latest on Linda today:
She had her eyes open for a bit this morning, don't know if what she is seeing is actually registering but at least the swelling has gone down considerably. Still heavily sedated and will be till after her surgery on her left leg, which is scheduled for tomorrow. The nurse said she had a comfortable night last night.

Her facial bruising is diminishing also, the black and blue is now sort of orange - yellow, almost all of the cuts have scabbed over.

She had a problem with the gunk & crud in the right lung's lower lobe. It didn't look good on an x-ray, so the sent a fiber optic camera down her lung to look at it, and then suctioned it all out. She seems to be breathing easier now.

Heartbeat 96-103
Respirations 6-9
O2 in the blood 96%
Blood pressure 99 over 64

So she seems to be slowly improving, she looks relaxed and not squirming around like she was Thurs and Fri.

Will let you all know how the surgery goes tomorrow. The kids are all fine, even Zach is adjusting to the sight of her, he had trouble with that a few days ago, but is doing a lot better now.

The results from today (4/14) are:

Heartbeat - 101
Respirations 9 - 16
Blood Oxygen Content 96%
Blood Pressure 116-131 over 71-89 ... All this means, she's
    doing good.

Now for the update: She is scheduled to have her ankle and muscle surgery for Monday.

-the vertebrae in her back has a burst fracture, but it is not compressing anything, she'll be getting a back brace to wear and she should heal up in about 3 months.

- doing good, had a peaceful night last night and all day today.

- she opened her eyes for a bit this morning, and is still responding to commands to move and wiggle fingers and toes.

- her "exhaust" functions are working fine, no blood and no problems there.

- her left lung is still collapsed and they are monitoring that. The right lower part has a small buildup of gunk, which they working to get rid of.

- her incision (which looks like and is about as long as Interstate 5) looks to be healing well, just a little drainage. They said all the staples will be pulled before she goes home.

So, she's getting outstanding care and is still heavily sedated but seems to be comfortable and obviously not in pain. The swelling has gone down in her face a good deal, losing the black and blue around her eyes, and her cuts are scabbing over, so far so good.

Take care and will keep you all updated.

4-15-02

Had to run to DMV, to get new tags and registration for the green truck for Chris to drive. Couldn't find what had been mailed. I reopened the business account since we found the missing checkbook. Updated Lorianne, so she would have the latest for the rest of the town.

And then headed for the Hospital. I've been putting out this email daily so your dad, Danny, Pat and Mary will know what's going on.

She had a peaceful night Sunday.

She went to surgery at 1:35 pm Monday and was out by 3:35.

- The ultra sound they did on her leg showed the muscle did not detach as they had thought earlier, but it had split open lengthwise in the lower part. Good news, so they did not operate, they will wait till she can talk and will test its range of movement, but they are pretty confident it will heal itself. So, we'll wait and see.

- On her ankle, the fractured fibula (smaller of the two lower leg bones is aligned well and they inserted two screws to pull both the tibia and fibula back together to their normal position. They have her in a cast to her knee and feel that in six weeks she'll be out of it.

Vitals, 90 minutes after surgery:

Heart rate 103

Respiration 9 - 16

Blood O2 99%

Blood Pressure 123/62

They are decreasing the output of the respirator because her breathing is improving, they will try to remove the tube from her throat Tues. afternoon if she continues to do well. The lower portion of the right lung (approx 10%) is still collapsed from the "gunk" they had removed Sunday, but are monitoring this and feel it will re-inflate before long. Chest tube drainage is decreasing, a couple more days and they'll remove that tube. She does seem to cough up some "gunk" on her own now, another good sign.

Her swelling has gone down a lot, color is looking good, bruising clearing up. The large bruise on her forehead above her nose is almost gone, bruising to the left side of forehead slowly disappearing and under her left eye is clearing up. The cut on her right hand, index finger knuckle, was stitched up and healing well. Abdominal incision is no longer draining and looks pretty good.

She is on reduced medication, so is in and out more frequently and is a little more active, opening her eyes (and seems to recognize me), squeezes my hand, nods her head when they staff is telling her something. Anxiety is there when she does come around because of the mouthful of appliances, but calms right down and drifts off to sleep again.

Late in the afternoon, they dressed her in her "turtle shell" (looks more like and ancient Roman Centurions breast plate and back plates), but it's her back brace to protect the fractured vertebrae.

So if the respirator tube comes out Tues. without complications, they will probably move her out of ICU sometime Wed.

Date: Tue, 16 Apr 2002 20:19:57 -0700

Hello all,

Well Linda had a good night last night. They quit the morphine pain killer and this morning started to reduce more the function of the respirator, but she had some problems with that, so they will keep her on it for another day or two. Everything else is doing good.

They have started another medication for pain that doesn't effect the respiratory system, which in turn will help strengthen her diaphragm muscles. She has developed a slight fever but the doctor isn't worried about it.

Vitals: Heartrate 96
Blood O2 98%

Respiration 14
Blood Pressure 115/62

She is more alert (looking around moving her arms and legs) since they have reduced the medicine and is a where of us in the room which increases her anxiety, so we left early today in order she would concentrate on resting which she really needs.

She is looking better everyday so hopefully tomorrow afternoon the hose will come out, but only when she's ready.

Once again, thanks from the whole family for your prayers and thoughts.

Date: Wed, 17 Apr 2002 21:58:58 -0700

Hello again all,

Linda settled down last night and had a great day today. She is "tolerating" the tube down her throat and working with it. She is breathing on her own, with the respirator supplying 40% oxygen (down from 50 yesterday) to assist her breathing. (typically we breath 27% oxygen daily)

Heart rate 95-97
Blood O2 98%
Respirations 11-14
Blood Pressure 104/72

The fever she had yesterday is gone.

A major improvement from yesterday, very alert, awakes at the slightest noise or voice. Not in pain, just uncomfortable and very irritable/frustrated went she can't communicate or we don't understand what she is wanting. (I never was any good at 40 questions!!!)

When she woke up this morning, the nurse said she was a little startled because she didn't know where she was, what had happened to her and knew nothing of the accident. So he explained some of what happened, how she got there, and a little of what is wrong with her.

The swelling is almost gone and her face is looking great, just slight discoloration around the left eye and cheek. She recognized all of us, answered questions with head nods, hand moves and squeezes, and was even winking at the boys.

She is able to write a little. Her first note was, "Zach?", wanting to know where Zach was. I explained he was OK and at home, which seemed to satisfy her. (She has a very special bond with Zach, as he does with her)

They are planning on pulling the tube out tomorrow if the progress she has made continues. (they have a scale they rate her on every few hours, where she was 30+ yesterday, she was 14 this afternoon and we are looking for her to be 5, the magic number to pull the tube.

Prayers work and she is getting better .... thank you all!!!!

Thu, 18 Apr 2002 21:10:18 -0700

Another great day!!! She hit the 5 on the scale this morning about 11:00, so they sat her up (45 degrees) and removed the breathing tube about 2:00 this afternoon. She is breathing fine, she is receiving oxygen but, she doesn't have the tube in her mouth. She is talking (very hoarse) but it's good to hear her.

She is very alert and was even cracking some jokes, when her voice gives out she has written a couple of notes. So she is doing fine, a little confused with the time, but to be expected considering the medication she been given. She is amazed she slept a whole week.

Her vitals are about the same .... good and steady. Cuts and bruises are healing and says she is not in pain - just bed bored!!!

The "spine guys" were suppose to be in checking out her neck this afternoon. The x-rays show no damage, but the want to touch and feel and see what she has to say. If all checks out, they'll remove the neck collar, which will really please her.

Prayers are working ..... thank you all!!!!!

Friday, April 19, 2002

Talked about her injuries, to let her know what was wrong:

Facial fracture
Burst vertabrea in her mid back
Split muscle in her left fore leg
Broken fibula
Her left ankle had to be screwed back together
She had her diaphram ruptured and repaired
Collapsed left lung
Three puncture wounds: one behind left eye, below her left jaw
    in her neck and in the top of her left shoulder.
Cut requiring stitches in her right hand
Bruised and numerous cuts and scratches.

Told her that she was cut out of the Bronco and airlifted to Harborview. She started joking about her first helicopter ride and didn't remember it.

I had to ask her the following questions, as I speculate from seeing the way the rear mat in the trailer is uprooted and all the cement in a jumbled pile of broken bags (we have pictures of it) up in the front part of the trailer compartment. (if all the bags were stacked in the front, they wouldn't have been in the mess they are now):

Me ... "Do you remember the accident?" Linda ... "No."
Me ... " What do you remember?" Linda ... "I had gone to lumber store and picked up the cement and turning on the highway (Hwy 20) to come home. Matt Mikos was coming over to help set the posts in the back."
Me ... "Who loaded the cement?" — Linda ..."The guys working in the yard at lumber yard."
Me ..."Did you tell them how to load it?" — Linda ..."No, they were suppose to know what they are doing."
Me ... "Where did they put it in the trailer?" Linda ..."Just inside the back doors."

Me ... "Did they go inside the trailer to load any of it?" Linda ... "No, they just reached in with it."

Me ... "Did they have you sign a waiver of any sort for the way the trailer was loaded?" — Linda .... "No, nothing."

Date: Sun, 21 Apr 2002 20:37:26 -0700

Well, Linda was moved from ICU to a private room Friday night. They have removed the neck brace, the hoses in her nose, and the "exhaust" hose. She is looking great, talking and joking around. She is not suppose to put any weight on her left leg and has used a walker a little bit. She will have to visit the dentist, she managed to chip lots of teeth, nothing seems too bad though ... we'll keep our fingers crossed.

Physical Therapy has her using a leg exerciser 10 -12 hours a day to strengthen the injured muscle and keep it pliable.

She is able to sit up and feed herself the "best delicacies" the hospital has to offer ...... she says it all tastes like crap!!!!

Jeremy and Randi brought Kayla in this afternoon and she painted Linda's toe and fingernails.

She is scheduled for tests the first part of the week so, we'll see what happens. She is doing really well and is anxious to get home as we are to get her here also.

So, thanks again for the kind thoughts and prayers. The doctor said when they first brought her in they had their doubts, she was in pretty bad shape, and to look at her now, 12 days later, they are amazed!!!!

I talked to Linda today about the accident again, (explaining what I saw in the trailer, the pile of broken bags of cement and the ways the way the rear mat was torn up) and my belief that the accident was due to the improper loading of the trailer on the part of lumber store. I really believe it is negligence on their part and we should consult with a lawyer. She agrees (even though we both have been opposed to suing for trivial reasons, in her case, however, we believe it to be justified as to the extent of the damage involved) and recommended we talk to an attorney, once she is up and about.

Date: Mon, 22 Apr 2002 22:31:21 –0700

Had an interview with Seattle news reporter, Deborah Horne, from KIRO 7 TV. She had seen the Whidbey News Times article, on the internet and asked if she could talk to us (a human interest story she is working on, wants to talk to us and the rescue crews on the island). It is suppose to air on the 11:00 news tonight, Jeremy is going to tape it. She has asked to do a follow-up interview with Linda in a few weeks, when Linda is ready to.

Well, I just got back from Harborview, and they have removed the chest drainage tube, stitches from the hand, staples from her abdomen (50 some) and put a new fiberglass cast on her left leg, hot pink, no less .... it goes good with the polish Kayla did her toe nails in, yesterday. Her spirits are good, she's talkative and getting restless from the "comfortable" hospital beds. Her voice is still a bit hoarse, but she sounds great to us.

THE DOCTORS ARE GOING TO SEND HER HOME TOMORROW AFTERNOON (Tues) as long as nothing develops overnight. She is ready to get out of there and relax.... without being poked or prodded every couple of minutes.

So, we are cleaning house and fluffing pillows for her.

God answers prayers!!! Thanks again to all

Date: Tuesday, 23 Apr 2002

Brought Linda home today!!!!! She is doing great and looks beautiful.

She had me wash her hair before checking out of the hospital, she wanted to look her best. (I sure hope that this is the best for her, meaning, we are so happy and excited for her to come home, but if there is any reason that she should stay in the hospital longer, then that's where she should be.) They briefed us on getting a blood test next week, back to Harborview in two weeks for a checkup, prescription for some pain pills (for her back), to use the leg exerciser for 10 hrs a day and if she has trouble breathing or shortness of breath to call 911 or the hospital. She can take the back brace off 1 hr a day, for cleaning and change of shirt.

A rough trip down there and back for me, must be all catching up with me or some bug, threw up a few times on the way down, and at the Mukilteo ferry crossing on the way back.

Thursday 25 Apr. 2002

Had to go out and rent a wheelchair, so we can get her around the house. She has jokingly said, "if I had known this was going to happen, I would have worked out and built up my upper body strength!!!"

Had another great day with Linda. She has sat on the front deck to get a little sun, Ron and Ann Willis stopped by for a chat. Linda expressed a desire to know what the Lord has in store for her, after all she went through. She said, "I love the Lord more today than before the accident, I wonder what he has in mind for me?"

We took her to town to get her hair done, she is in such good spirits, **it's great to have her home.**

Several people have dropped by the house to visit her, Ron and Anne Willis, Patty and Laura Henderson, the Chambers, Gayle Larson, Linda Busic and her daughter, Dennis Terry, and others whose names escape me at the moment. When asked how she feels, her typical smiling answer is "well, I've felt better, but then I've felt a lot worse, so I'm doing OK."

She says she is still planning on meeting me in England in June or July (that is, if the doctors allow her to travel). She wants to bring Ashley and Zach so we can all get with Chris and see the sites.

Friday 26 April 2002

My love for Linda is indescribable; I'm continually amazed at her cheerfulness after all she's been through. I don't mind the least in helping her and caring for her. It is enjoyable to help her in her needs since she is so limited in what she can do. God has truly blessed me with this beautiful woman. **I'm really looking forward to growing old on the porch with her**. As always, I'm dreading the thought of having to leave and go back to work in a couple of weeks. But our plans are for me to work for five more years and retire after I turn 55.

Our sacrifice now will be rewarded then, the house will be paid off, we'll have a nice savings account and we can start the doing some short term mission trips that we have thought about for years.

Helping her get around the house, seems to be doing better each day.

Sat, 27 Apr 2002 06:07:55 -0700

It is a sad day for us all, Linda has gone home to be with the Lord. She passed away earlier this morning unexpectedly.

More a bit later, just a sincere thank you for all your prayers and kind thoughts.

John and family

She said she was having trouble breathing when I checked on her this morning (was sleeping fine about 90 minutes earlier), and wanted to lay in the bed with the brace off. As I was calling 911, she said she couldn't breath, gave the phone to Chris and started CPR and continued to the fire department arrived about 15 minutes later. They took over CPR and took her to Whidbey General. The doctor came out after a few, saying it doesn't look good but wants to try something else. About 10 minutes later he came out with the sad news. They let me in to see her for a minute, kissed her goodbye and went out to meet Chris in the parking lot. Went home to tell the kids and Marion, and then called Jeremy.

Called Lee and Mary, the Chambers, the Hendersons and Barb Early.

The coroner came by the house this afternoon and gave me her wedding ring, said that a massive blood clot formed in her leg, broke loose, traveled up and blocked her heart and lungs, there was nothing anyone could have done.

I can remember at different weddings we had gone to, the minister would describe the symbolism of the ring, gold the most precious of metals, so you should consider each other as most precious, round and never ending. As I sat and held her ring, originally it held five diamonds, now there were only four, one each for our children and the missing one for the child we lost. Like gold, Linda was most precious to me and to our children, round and without end, like our never-ending love for each other.

I am so thankful that the Lord allowed us a couple of great days with her before He took her home to Heaven. I really miss her as will the all the kids and Kayla, she wasn't just my wife and mother to us but was also our best friend.

Things I will miss:

Our praying together in bed at night.
Watching and listening to her sing at church.

Her strength in her faith and trust in the Lord. Always one to give Him the praise. (I remember the first comment Linda made when our long awaited daughter, Ashley, was born. The doctor said, "it's a girl" {we had prayed a long time for a baby girl}, and she promptly replied, "Thank you, Jesus!". I noticed how this also got the attention of all the hospital staff in the delivery room.)

Her advice that she always freely gave me (whether I asked for it or not, but then, she always had a good sense of judgment, and I always valued her opinion.)

Her companionship, just being with her. Evenings together, watching a movie, a walk around the neighborhood, watching the sunset at the beach, playing cards in the lodge while the kids were skiing/snowboarding. Just a fun person to be with.

Her diligence, when she started something, she saw it through to completion. (Several years ago, I decided to try to find my birthmother, since I had been adopted at birth. It took several years, but thanks to Linda, who did the majority of the research, I talked to my birthmother on my fortieth birthday for the first time.)

Even with all the separations we've had over the years, we always kept our anniversary special. While I was in Bosnia, each year when we weren't together, I'd get an anniversary cake and shared it with our local host country employees who seemed to think it was a little odd, but they loved it. Each year after that, they would start hinting about the beginning of August "about time to get a cake". They probably thought "very strange, this American!!!"

Our morning trips to *Chocolates for Breakfast*, a local espresso shop, where Linda used to work for a time before I went overseas. Just enjoying her company, sometimes working the daily crossword puzzle with her, and other times just talking with friends.

Our honeymoon was cut short when Linda developed an impacted wisdom tooth, the second day of our married life. Over the following years in the military and raising the children we never had any real time away, just the two of us. While I worked in Bosnia, I had an R&R every three to four months, so Linda would drive up to Vancouver, B.C. and we would spend a couple of days alone together before heading home. These mini-honeymoons were ever so great, and I believe, strengthened our marriage even more. Over the years, our commitment to each other allowed us to be so open with one another, we could talk about anything without fear of embarrassment.

In our many wanderings, we'd often find a place to sit and enjoy our favorite pastime together …. "people watching".

The pride and joy she took in our family. She had a unique and special bond with each of the children and as they married, she bonded with their spouses. Kayla reminds me almost every time I see her how she "misses grandma Cookie, but she's an angel in Heaven now, you know."

The joy she would have shared with our daughter, Ashley, who at the time of this writing, is deeply involved with the planning of her own upcoming wedding.

Her favorite holiday was Christmas. She loved decorating the house, shopping for gifts, and enjoying our own family traditions. Christmas morning ahs traditionally began with the reading of Luke 2:1-20 and then followed with our family praying together, each thanking the Lord for his blessings in our lives. The joy of passing out the gifts, relaxing and enjoying the day as a family, and our own family tradition ….. a big pot of her homemade chili and cornbread. Christmas's haven't been the same, but we rejoice in knowing she is sharing the day and celebrating with our Lord.

Some memories

When we were dating each other, she stopped by the house to show me some "police moves" they had been taught at school during a women's defense class. Now she was 5'4" and I am 6'7". So she proceeded to demonstrate these various tactics, which didn't have the affect she was looking for. So as the years passed she would threaten me with her dangerous police moves!!!

While stationed in Massachusetts, our daughter Ashley, was born with severe nerve damage to her left arm, which left it basically hanging limp at her side. We were referred to a specialist at Children's Hospital in Boston who prescribed a lengthy routine of physical therapy. Linda faithfully worked with Ashley daily over the next few years. With this and we believe, with a lot of prayers, her arm slowly began to function and she achieved 80% mobility in that time. By the time she was four, she had complete use of her arm and no further complications.

She always had the ability to laugh at herself. When our son Christopher was born, his face was really chubby. He had slits for eyes because of his fat little cheeks, and he had scratched his face up pretty good. A couple of days later, she had strolled to the maternity ward infant viewing window and was just gazing at our son. A woman and her mother came up to the window, next to her. While admiring their 'perfect' baby, the mother pointed to Chris and remarked, "the poor little thing, isn't that the ugliest baby you've ever seen?" With tears in her eyes, she went back to her room and cried up a storm. In later years, she would laugh over the incident and comment on how well he turned out, even when "a crazy lady" thought he was so ugly.

When we transferred from the east coast to the west coast, we were passing through Kingman, Arizona. We had stopped and had lunch at a Wendy's restaurant. As we were all getting back into the van, Linda slid into her seat and somehow managed to impale her "back side" on a toothpick. Now she had to drop her slacks a bit so I could remove the object. Now she was a bit embarrassed, understandably, this happening in a public parking lot, but she got the biggest kick at seeing the kids both embarrassed and laughing to no end over what had just happened.

Linda and Ashley had gone to the grocery store and while roaming the aisles, Linda had picked up a toilet bowl brush. While thinking of what else she needed and tapping the brush against her shoulder, when it tangled up in her hair. So she asked her daughter for help and Ashley quickly walked away saying something about " not knowing this crazy, obviously, disturbed woman who keeps following her". After the two manage to cover a few aisles (in hysterics), the brush was untangled and they finished their shopping.

Photo by John
Linda and Ashley were like sisters most of the time. The two would borrow each other's clothes, shoes and jewelry. Linda would occasionally dress the same as Ashley and then tease her

about being twins. I took this picture on one of my R&R trips from Bosnia at Whistler Mountain in British Columbia, because Ashley was playfully accusing 'Mumsy', of copying her style.

Shortly after meeting my birthmother I contacted my brother, Danny, for the first time. Linda had decided to surprise me by arranging for us to meet him a few weeks later when we flew to Colorado and spent a great weekend together with his family. We all have shared a special relationship ever since. Linda and Danny both loved to playfully torment each other to no end.

Photo by John
This was Linda, not one to put on a false front, or pretend to be someone she wasn't. At home in her jeans, sneakers, denim jacket or a vest and with her ever present smile. I took this picture there, and it has become my favorite one of her .... a beautiful day, with a beautiful woman.

"But from the beginning of the creation,
God made them male and female.
For this reason a man shall leave his father
and mother and be joined to his wife,

59

and the two shall become one flesh;
so then they are no longer two, but one flesh."

Mark 10:6-8

My most favorite memories of her what was to be our last summer together. She had flown to Zurich, Switzerland where we were to meet and celebrate our 28th wedding anniversary. I had flown to Zurich from Zagreb, Croatia, after convoying out of Bosnia. The first four days there, it had rained everyday except this Sunday morning. We had taken the train to Schaffhausen, a quiet little town up near the German border. We found a little café along the Rhine River and sat sharing an order of fries, people watching and admiring the scenery. A little old gentleman joined us for about a half an hour, because no other tables were empty. (We couldn't understand his German and he didn't speak English, but he seemed to enjoy himself) Linda and I just talked of future plans and how we had been blessed throughout our married life together.

Approximately 22 years ago Linda and I started this lengthy, involved process of trying to locate my birthparents and the circumstances leading to my adoption. In December 2004, I completed the task when I found that my "birth-father", who had died in 1965, had a son, Ron, who was raised as an only child. As Linda had done a tremendous amount of research, I am sorry that she was not able to be there when the three of us brothers, met in person for the first time. In September 2004, we have found that there is another brother and sister to add to our family that fit in between the oldest Ron and the youngest, being myself.

Photo by Carol Witherspoon
This photo is of the tree brothers meeting for the first time, a lot of the work and effort that made this possible was done by Linda.

Our Children's Memories

Zachary's Memories

Mom was also my home-school teacher. The best memories of her are when she took me snowboarding on Wednesdays during the winter. It was a lot of fun boarding and skiing with her. She was always cutting jokes and we would laugh together. We talked about all kinds of things on the way up the mountain. My friends would go with us sometimes and they all liked her because she was cool, not just a mom but, a real friend. She was always there for me.

Ashley's Memory

Mom was more of a sister and best friend to me, together we were a team with my horse competition, she was always there for me. My only wish is that she could have been there for my wedding day.

Photo by Jeremy Cook
This empty chair was set near the altar, in memory of my mom.
A rose and her bible a rested on the seat.

This is from my wedding program (August 21, 2004):

Well, my little girl's twenty-three
I walk her down the asile
It's a shame her mom can't be here now
To see her lovely smile.
They throw the rice, I catch her eye
As the rain starts coming down.
She takes my hand and says,
"Daddy don't be sad, Cause I know Momma's
watching now"

And there's holes in the floor of Heaven
And her tears are pouring down,
That's how you know she's watching,
Wishing she could be here now.
And sometimes when I'm lonely,
I remember she can see.
Yes, there's holes in the floor of heaven,
And she's watching over you and me.....

By Steve Wariner

I would like to take a moment to remember a very special person, my mother Linda Joyce Cook. Her chair here today may only be occupied by her Bible and a rose, but she is not gone .... her presence is felt by those she loved and she will never be forgotten.

Although she can't be here today to celebrate with us, I know she is watching down on us, smiling and laughing like she loved to do.

I love you mom! - your baby girl

Jeremy, My Memories of Mom

I am writing this to let everyone know what a wonderful person my mom is. I will always love her and miss her. Not a day goes by that I don't think about her. She is the best Mom and Grandma that any child could ever ask for.

Grandma Cookie was my daughter, Kayla's, best friend. No one could ask for a more loving and fun grandma. I remember Mom would sometimes call up out of the blue and ask if she could come down and take Kayla for a couple days, to hang out at grandma's house. Sometimes those days turned into over a week and Kayla did not want to come home because she was having so much fun at "Grandma Cookie's house". When she returned we would hear about all the ice cream and McDonald's that she got to have with Grandma. After all, isn't that what grandmas are for. I only wish that our other two children, Parker and Alexa, could have met their "Grandma Cookie".

I am going to share some of my memories of Mom from when I was growing up. I will never forget the day when (I think I was 8) when my mom reached to the back seat of the car to swat me with a wooden spoon. Upon contact, the spoon broke in half. I remember her anger turning into laughter in a split second.

There was also a time, during one of our cross-country trips, that we stopped for lunch and while returning to the car we heard a scream from mom. Come to find out, when she sat down, she had sat on a toothpick. So there we were, in the parking lot of a restaurant with my mom with her pants down and my dad pulling a tooth pick out of her backside. My brother, sister and I thought that was the funniest thing.

After I got married and had had our first child, we started taking family vacations with my parents. We would all meet in Whistler B.C every 6 months or so. I remember sitting out on the deck one night just talking to my mom and telling jokes. I don't remember what I said, but she started laughing so hard that she could not get out of her chair and make a quick trip to the bathroom. Then we really had something to laugh about.

On one of our trips to Whistler, my parents decided to go bar hopping with my wife and I. Let me preface this by saying that my parents never went to bars or even drank, for that matter that I could recall. So when my mom wanted to go out with us, I thought it was the coolest thing. When we arrived at the bar, we ordered some drinks and just hung out, wondering what the cage on the dance floor was for. Then a bachelorette party came in and put it to good use. You should have seen the look on Mom's face. I couldn't figure out if the look was from watching those girls in that cage or from the two double long island ice teas that she had just drank. But it was priceless.

I just wanted to share a few of my best memories of my mom. She was a wonderful person that always had a smile on her face (except for when I was in high school). I know that everyone knows what a great person she was and I hope that we all cherish her memory.

I love you, mom ...... Jeremy

Christopher's Memories

My loving mother Linda J. Cook, You are and forever, will be missed by every person who had the chance to meet you.

About a year after my mothers' death, my dad asked me to write down a few memories of my mom for this book he was writing. As usual I have procrastinated. So here we are in Feb of 2008 finally doing what dad asked me to do. If I were still a child and waited this long to do what I was asked, mom would have grounded me for sure.

Like my father, I decided at a young age to serve my country and joined the U.S. Air Force. Almost 13 years later, I find myself writing my memories of my mother on my second tour of duty in Iraq and sixth tour to the mid-east. The first four were while mom was alive, but I will get to those memories later. "Why now?" I ask myself. I think it was just one of those days everyone has. Just about everything that could go wrong, has gone wrong. Just about every person who could annoy me, has done just that. Even though I am married and have a wife who like mom (dads best friend), is my best friend, I found that I would give just about anything to talk to my mom today. So leaving work, I found myself going straight back to my room for bed.

Lying in bed I decided to finally read what everyone else has said about mom. I found it funny that most of the comical memories are already mention by my siblings, especially since I have grown apart from my brothers and sister over the years. The comical memories of my mom show me that she was the center of our family and held us all together. Everyone who knows our family knows that Jeremy and I have never had the closest relationship. It is no secret. Before I go any farther I want to thank Jeremy for everything he did when mom first had her accident. If he had not acted quickly and took the initiative to contact everyone, I may not have been able to see mom one last time. Thank you, Jeremy.

It is ironic that even though we are not close, Jeremy is part of my earliest memory of mom. Mom was inside the house (the little red house on 600 Ave) talking on the phone, while Jeremy and I had climb onto the roof of the house any were jumping off into the back yard. Mom came outside screaming at us that we could break our legs or worse our necks. That is my earliest memory of her, getting yelled and into trouble with my big brother. We could not have been any older than six and eight years old.

In the seventh grade, I began home schooling. In the public system, my grades were terrible….C's, D's and F's. I was reading at a third grade level, and failing math because I couldn't understand anything more than simple addition and subtraction. Mom sorted me out. She became my teacher. With a newborn baby (Zach) and Ashley, who was only about four or five years old, she took on the job getting me up to speed. She would spend hours with my at the dinning room table doing math. Starting with the simple problems, we worked on them until I thoroughly understood them. In less than a year she had me working at a 7th grade level on every subject.

Mom was always there for me in high school as well. Even though I didn't attend the actual city school, she made sure that Ashley and I and later Zach, all acquired the same social skills as any other kid. She made sure we got involved in church groups and different activities through a local home school association. Because of that I received the social skills and mom also got to play the match maker. Yes, I know this sounds weird, but my mom hooked me up with my first girlfriend, Stephanie. She was also home schooled, and our mothers got to be good friends. As time went on mom encouraged me to ask Stephanie on a date, since there seemed to be a natural chemistry between us. Both moms were happy as were both kids. Then a couple months down the road, once again my wonderful mom was there for me when the girls' dad caught up with me in town, and made it very clear that I was not to see his daughter again. No reason was given, however with a threat, he made it clear. Mom was there and got me through my first broken heart.

Fast forward a about a year or so, when I had graduated from school and started junior college, and subsequently stop attending classes I realized I was going no where and started thinking about the military. So, I went and talked to the different recruiters. The Marines did not appeal to me, and as for the Navy, I didn't want to be stuck on a boat for six months with just guys for company. I was toying with both the Air Force and the Army. I remember talking with my close friends, Jessaca McMurdo (then Andrews), and she suggest that I not join the Army, and if I must join the military, to join the Air Force. Thank you Jess, that advice, upon all the other advice over the many years was spot on. So I talk to the recruiter some more, then told mom about my plans. One day out of the blue, I said "Mom, I have decided to join the Air Force." She was shocked at first, but once the shock wore off, she was 100% supportive of my choice and my career until her death.

She was as supportive of my career as any mother could be. When she came to Lackland A.F.B. Texas for my graduation from basic training, I new she was proud. She brought Grandma Stone (her mom) and my kid brother Zach with her to see me at the first major milestone of my adult life. She saw where I trained, ate, lived, and learned about life in the military. She even embarrassed me while looking at my wall locker with all my uniforms hanging starched and pressed, shirts and underwear folded in neat six inch squares and everything neatly in it place. As she was standing there in awe of how tidy my area was, my TI (Training Instructor) walked up. After I did the customary introductions, mom thanked him for getting me to "keep my room clean" like she had tried to for the past 19 years. Yes, I caught hell from the TI about that.

10 months later she once again supported me while I was on my first deployment to Kuwait. While deployed she graciously took control of all my finances, her argument was that it would be one less thing for me to worry about, so I could focus on my job and staying safe. When I got back four months later, she managed to save me about $3000 of my own money. Three months after returning from that trip to Kuwait, I went back to Kuwait for a second time. Once again she took care of everything for me while I was away. She did this each time I deployed over the next two years. On the second trip to Kuwait, I spent my first Christmas away from my family. She made sure that even though my friends (who she had never met) and I were on the other side of the world; we would have a tree and presents to open. She even sent me a copy of " T'was the night Before Christmas" in hopes of me carrying on the family traditional reading on Christmas Eve. She also made sure that I had at least a letter a week. Those who have never been so far away from

family and loved ones for so long, have no idea how much a letter from mom can boost a soldiers morale, but mom knew. At least once a month I knew mom would have a care package in the mail. Each package always contained her letter, the (very comical) police blotters from the local newspaper and a note saying "make sure you share the goodies with the rest of the boys". A couple of years ago, in England, my new boss was one of those boys from Kuwait. The first thing he asked me was does mom still sent me the home made cookies and the newspaper clippings? He ensured a collection was taken at work and flowers were sent out when mom passed.

So mom took care of her boy and others moms' boys while there were off in distant lands. After my fourth deployment, I came home for Christmas and I brought home the girlfriend! I think I was more nervous than the girl. I didn't tell mom I was bringing her with me for the holidays. Well, those of you who were fortunate to ever know my mom know exactly what she did. She welcomed my girlfriend as if she were one of her own children. I proposed to my girlfriend, who said yes, and then couple of days after Christmas, mom sat us down talked to us about a healthy marriage and how to make it work and the importance of a long engagement. We didn't listen. The marriage lasted under a year, but that was the best thing that ever could have happened.

My divorce was hard. At first, I didn't want to tell mom that I was getting a divorce. I did not want to tell her that I failed at the one thing her and dad always put forth 100% and that I had not listened to the advice she gave us. So I talked to the only other person I new I could talk to, my life long friend Jessaca. She told me to "tell mom" and that "mom" would understand. Wouldn't you know, once again Jess was right. A couple of days later mom and I were at lunch, just the two of us. She looked at me and asked, "When did you two decide to end your marriage?" So I told her everything. She gave me the best advice and then said that if it is truly over then it was for the best and there must be someone else I was meant to be with.

A few years later I was stationed in England, but was attending a school at Lackland again, when mom and Ashley came to visit me for a weekend. As with Jeremy's memory of mom in a bar in Whistler, I too was absolutely floored when mom asked if there are any decent bars that Ashley could get into being under 21. No there wasn't. So either way we enjoyed the weekend shopping and catching up. I don't quite remember where we were or why Ashley wasn't with us, but mom looked at me and said your going to marry this girl aren't you? Obviously she was referring to my wonderful wife Ixcheal. We had not been dating long at the time and started off as friends before dating. Mom had spoken to Ixcheal many times over the phone and even though she and Ixcheal never got to meet in person, they got along from the start. I of course told that I definitely thought Ixcheal was the person that I was meant to be with. Mom then told me that she was very fond Ixcheal and thought she would continue to make the happiest man I could be. I think it is amazing mom could tell that kind of thing without ever meeting somebody face to face. This time I listened to moms' advice. I took things slow. Unfortunately mom never got to meet Ixcheal or Elis and Dylan (my stepsons).

Roughly two months after that wonderful weekend Ashley and I had with mom in Texas, I got the phone call from Jeremy about the accident. I was on the next available flight, courtesy of Jeremy's mother-in-law. Ixcheal and her family immediately assisted with anything and everything they could for me in England and I was back in Seattle at mom's side about 30 hrs after Jeremy's phone call. I am not going to go into all the memories of the visits to the hospital. I do remember the afternoon mom sat out on the porch after she was released from the hospital. She asked me when she gets to meet Ixcheal and the rest of her family. I told her that as soon as she was better and ready to travel she had come see us. She told me she could tell Ixcheal made me happy and it would be an honor to have Ixcheal as a daughter. I knew that Ixcheal also loved mom even though they had never met and has since commented several times that they did something right raising me the way they did.

Mom was my best friend, the only way a mom can be. She was my teacher, my leader, and my mentor. She treated everyone she came in contact with love and respect. She taught me many things in life. The most important though, is how to love. Both mom and dad taught me how to make a marriage work, even across the many miles apart and the days away from one another. I thank you both for your lessons and support in life.

I started this out a couple of hours ago mad as hell in Iraq, wishing I could talk to my mom almost six years after her death. Talking with her would have calmed me down. I find it amusing that after thinking of all memories of mom, I don't really remember why I was mad in the first place.

Mom, you are simply amazing!
I love you and miss you!

In Closing:

Photo by Lynette Tompkins
Sitting and watching the beautiful sunsets were always special
times for us, one of Linda's favorite things to do. Living on an
island in the Pacific Northwest provided us with this opportunity
on a more than regular basis, it was something we never tired of,
the splendor and beauty of God's creations never ceased to amaze
us. Many times were spent wondering what the Lord had planned
for us in the future.

The following was her favorite verse:

"For I know the thoughts that I think toward you," says the Lord, "thoughts of peace and not of evil, to give you a future and a hope. Then you will call upon Me and go and pray to Me and find Me, when you search for Me with all your heart."

Jeremiah 29:11-13

Life is short and one never knows when the Lord will decide it is time for one to go home, so live life to the fullest. Don't put off telling and doing things with loved ones, you may not get a second chance. For married couples, I can tell you the pain of losing your spouse is tremendous but the memories are always there, thankfully, the good far exceed the bad. I encourage you to work at keeping the marriage strong and sacred. Don't let self-pride get in the way of hampering your relationship with your spouse. Don't let yourself say "down the road sometime", I wish I would have said this, or done that, or hugged him/her more often, before they passed away.

God bless.

[i] "Libbey Hill Accident Victim Dies", The Coupeville Examiner, 3 May 2002
[ii] "Selfridge Navy plane down, 16 die", The Macomb Daily, October 7, 1978

Part II (A Couples Workbook)

Communication is an extremely important part of a marriage. If one cannot talk to the other about a problem or situation, anger and resentment tends to build up inside one of the partners. If this continues over a period of time, this will inevitably lead to more and larger problems.

No matter how long you have been married and think you know each other, changes happen. (For instance, Linda had always like gold jewelry. A few years ago when working overseas, I was planning on getting her a gift and I did what all men do, called and asked my daughter what Linda would like. I passed along that I was thinking of getting, either a gold bracelet or necklace. Ashley informed me, and very directly that, "Mom really likes silver…" and there was one she had her eye on. The same thing happened with her taste in music. I had come home on an R&R, and my family was now listening to country music, something they hadn't had an interest in before.) So, I realize that we all change and most cases, without prior notice.

The intention for this section of the book is to get the two of you to talk to each other. The procedure is fairly simple, the wife will respond in writing after the question on the page annotated <u>Her Answers</u> (in the upper right hand corner of the page). The husband will respond on the page annotated <u>His Answers</u>.

Note to the men: *Now I have always been of the belief, that a man is as good as his word. In the day of our grandfathers, and a practice still common in many areas of the world even today, men will finalize an agreement or deal with a simple of* *the shake of the hand. So I am going to assume each husband will shake my hand (in spirit), thus agreeing not to look as his wife's response until he has completed his own.*

Why that way? I believe each of you should honestly answer each question without any prompting or persuasion from the other's answer. Since there is no right or wrong answer, so there is really no need to peek. (And one more thing men, a simple yes or no isn't going to hack it, you'll have to expand on your answer ..... women are stickers for detail!!!)

Once you both have answered the question, you may read each other's response.

Ground rules:

1. This is an exercise in love and learning, so the two of you arrange some time alone, (where you hopefully won't get interrupted) and go over the answers. Do one or two questions at a time, since this isn't a college entrance exam, there is no time limit, take whatever time you need.

2. You are to discuss differences in the answers in a loving manner. Try to examine why you each see something differently. Remember the basic difference between men and women:

Men think logically and women think emotionally.

3. When you talk to each other, look into each other's eyes, not over the shoulder or down at the floor. As a couple you two share a special intimacy, so you should be able to talk freely about any subject without fear of embarrassment or shame.

Remember you two are in love with each other, so you're not to hold a grudge against one another if you didn't hear the answer you expected, as I mentioned earlier .... "changes happen". This is why you should discuss these in a loving manner. You will learn more about that someone you've agreed to share your life with. ***Good luck and have fun!!!***

Since this is the first, let's call this a warm-up.

What is your wife's favorite:

Flowers?

Color?

Perfume (hers)/cologne (his)?

Son?

Recording Artist?

Movie?

Bible verse?

Place to kiss?

Food?

Restaurant?

His Answers Cont.

Some questions but about your husband:

Football team?

Color?

Perfume (hers)/cologne (his)?

Song?

Recording Artist?

Movie?

Bible verse?

Place to kiss?

Food?

Restaurant?

Her Answers Cont.

<u>His Answers</u>

Now, that wasn't very hard, was it? How did the two of you do?

The rest will take some time and some thought, so don't hurry.

What are your goals for the next five years, ten years, and if you have even thought of it, how about retirement age? Take in to account your children if the of you two have any.

In the Bible, Proverbs 31: 10-31, describe women as a source of energy, strength, vision and a hard worker. In Genesis, man and woman are described as "help meets" (helpmate) to each other. I believe this to mean that spouses are to compliment the other, assisting, helping and supporting in a way to complete each other, as in strengthening weak areas.

How do you support each other in reaching these goals?

If you haven't planned that far, what would you see as possible goals and what support is needed?

His Answers Cont.

<u>Her Answers</u>

How do you think the two of you did?

The rest will take some time and some thought, so don't hurry.

What are your goals for the next five years, ten years, and if you have even thought of it, how about retirement age? Take in to account your children if the of you two have any.

In the Bible, Proverbs 31: 10-31, describe women as a source of energy, strength, vision and a hard worker. In Genesis, man and woman are described as "help meets" (helpmate) to each other. I believe this to mean that spouses are to compliment the other, assisting, helping and supporting in a way to complete each other, as in strengthening weak areas.

How do you support each other in reaching these goals?

If you haven't planned that far, what would you see as possible goals and what support is needed?

Her Answers Cont.

What are you wife's strengths?

How about weaknesses?

What are your fears?

How do you or would you help the other in overcoming these?

His Answers Cont.

<u>Her Answers</u>

What are you husband's strengths?

How about weaknesses?

What are your fears?

How do you or would you help the other in overcoming these?

Her Answers Cont.

<u>His Answers</u>

Being former military and later, working overseas as a contractor, Linda and I had spent allot of time apart. In our younger days, mail and a few phone calls (which tended to be expensive back then) were about the only means of keeping in contact with each other. Later, I started keeping a journal, which I would leave with her to read when I was home. *(Some good friends of ours, Roy and Carol S., each keep a journal when they are apart. They've been doing this since he was a young naval pilot in Vietnam and continue, even today, as he is now an airline pilot. They exchange journals with each other on the next separation, to read each other's thoughts, write occasional responses and record new entries.)*

When you are separated, how do you keep in touch with each other?

How important is this communication to your spouse and why? *(There are some couples, I've known, who are apart and have very little contact during these periods, which seem to work for them, according to one side. Now, not having talked to the other spouse, I don't know their feeling.)*

Are you satisfied with your particular situation or is there a need for improvement?

What do you think would or works best for the two you?

When you are apart, how do you keep in touch with each other?

How important is this communication to your spouse and why? *(There are some couples, I've known, who are apart and have very little contact during these periods, which seem to work for them, according to one side. Now, not having talked to the other spouse, I don't know their feeling.)*

Are you satisfied with your particular situation or is there a need for improvement?

What do you think would or works best for the two of you?

<u>His Answers</u>

Describe your idea of a romantic evening (his). *(For sake of embarrassment, if your children should ever happen to read your responses ……….. care should exercised in answering this question!!!! Some details you may want to discuss only and not put in writing.)*

His Answers Cont.

<u>Her Answers</u>

Describe your idea of a romantic evening (hers). *(For sake of embarrassment, if your children should ever happen to read your responses ……….. care should exercised in answering this question!!!! Some details you may want to discuss only and not put in writing.)*

Her Answers Cont.

What was your most memorable time together?

What made this memory so special?

His Answers Cont.

<u>Her Answers</u>

What was your most memorable time together?

What made this memory so special?

Her Answers Cont.

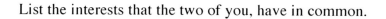

<u>His Answers</u>

List the interests that the two of you, have in common.

In the last month, how many have you two, as a couple, participated in?

His Answers Cont.

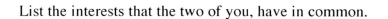

List the interests that the two of you, have in common.

In the last month, how many have you two, as a couple, participated in?

Her Answers Cont.

<u>His Answers</u>

How much time do you two spend together a week? Now, we're not counting sleeping, just time the two of you are alone with each other to talk, relax, or just enjoy each other's company alone, free of distractions and disturbances.

What are some of the reasons you don't spend more time together?

His Answers Cont.

How much time do you two spend together a week? Now, we're not counting sleeping, just time the two of you are alone with each other to talk, relax, or just enjoy each other's company alone, free of distractions and disturbances.

What are some of the reasons you don't spend more time together?

Try to come up with some ideas, on how you two can spend some time alone each week (i.e. a dinner date, a movie night, an evening out, a walk in the park, etc.)

Her Answers Cont.

Since I was in the navy, I flew aircrew, which was considered hazardous duty, and with the loss of our squadron aircraft, as mentioned earlier, Linda and I had discussed what the other should do, if one of us ever happen to pass away before the other. We both agreed that if the right individual came along, we would want the other to remarry, since we both enjoyed being married.

Have the two of you ever discussed this area?

Have you ever discussed about what would happen if one or both of you died suddenly?

Do you have a will prepared?

Who would you want to raise your children?

Do you know your spouse's funeral wishes? (*We had talked about this a few times over the years and it was allot easier when that sad day arrived.*)

His Answers Cont.

Have the two of you ever discussed this area?

Have you ever discussed about what would happen if one or both of you died suddenly?

Do you have a will prepared?

Who would you want to raise your children?

Do you know your spouse's funeral wishes? (*We had talked about this a few times over the years and it was allot easier when that sad day arrived.*)

Her Answers Cont.

His Answers

When Linda died, one thing that I suddenly became aware of and was not the least bit prepared for, were the household finances. She had always handled the finances since it always seemed that I was off flying, TDY or on assignment somewhere away from home. (She didn't really appreciate my "check booking technique" when we got married, and she was always better at math, so she always took care of that part.)

Do you discuss the finances with each other? *(This is typically the most volatile subject in a marriage, but it also, a fact of life, bills have to be paid.)*

Do you both know where all of your important papers are, and do you both have access to all bank accounts? *(Linda had started a retail business and the account was in her name (since I was overseas), one never knows when the Lord will take someone home, so I think she probably would have added my name later, but didn't get around to it. She had a car, licensed and titled in her name, both of these presented some problems when it came time to settle her affairs.)*

His Answers Cont.

<u>Her Answers</u>

When Linda died, one thing that I suddenly became aware of and was not the least bit prepared for, were the household finances. She had always handled the finances since it always seemed that I was off flying, TDY or on assignment somewhere away from home. (She didn't really appreciate my "check booking technique" when we got married, and she was always better at math, so she always took care of that part.)

Do you discuss the finances with each other? *(This is typically the most volatile subject in a marriage, but it also a fact of life, bills have to be paid.)*

Do you both know where all of your important papers are, and do you both have access to all bank accounts? *(Linda had started a retail business and the account was in her name (since I was overseas), one never knows when the Lord will take someone home, so I think she probably would have added my name later, but didn't get around to it. She had a car, licensed and titled in her name, both of these presented some problems when it came time to settle her affairs.)*

<u>Her Answers Cont.</u>

This is going to be a hard question, but honesty is one of the basic foundations of a healthy marriage.

How would you rate your relationship with your spouse? And why?

What area(s) do you feel need work?

If counseling would help, would you go together? (*Now, I'm not saying everyone needs outside help, but sometimes if an issue is at an impasse, a trained third party may be the key to resolving that problem.*) If no, then, why not?

Is the word "forgive", used frequently in your marriage?

As a couple, how is your spiritual growth?

Who is the spiritual head in your marriage?

<u>Her Answers</u>

How would you rate your relationship with your spouse? And why?

What area(s) do you feel need work?

If counseling would help, would you go together? *(Now, I'm not saying everyone needs outside help, but sometimes if an issue is at an impasse, a trained third party may be the key to resolving that problem.)* If no, then, why not?

Is the word "forgive", used frequently in your marriage?

As a couple, how is your spiritual growth?

Who is the spiritual head in your marriage?

<u>His Answers</u>

What first attracted you to your wife?

His Answers Cont.

<u>Her Answers</u>

What first attracted you to your husband?

Her Answers Cont.

What do you find that attracts you to your wife today?

His Answers Cont.

<u>Her Answers</u>

What do you find that attracts you to your husband today?

Her Answers Cont.

<u>His Answers</u>

In a recent sermon, Dr. Allan Stirling talked about **relational struggles**, " ... that cause missionaries to leave their field assignments prematurely, throw in the towel on a job, or in a relationship with a friend or even in a marriage". These could be differences with fellow missionaries, local workers, family, schooling, etc.

What relational struggles do you see affecting your marriage?

How well do each of you interact with your spouses parents/family?

Are there friends that annoy your spouse and if so, why?

Are there some issues with parents or friends that seem to constantly interfere with your relationship?

<u>Her Answers</u>

What relational struggles do you see affecting your marriage?

How well do each of you interact with your spouses parents/family?

Are there friends that annoy your spouse and if so, why?

Are there some issues with parents or friends that seem to constantly interfere with your relationship?

His Answers

Now, I am going to step out of the comfort zone, which in turn passes on to you. What one thing does your wife do, that annoys the daylights out of you?

(**Note to men**: handle this one very delicately, carefully choose your words and remember, when the Lord created all the women on this planet, only 8 were meant to be Victoria Secret models!!!)

<u>His Answers Cont.</u>

Her Answers

Now, I am going to step out of the comfort zone, which in turn passes on to you. What one thing does your husband do, that annoys the daylights out of you?

Her Answers Cont.

<u>His Answers</u>

I Corinthians 13:4-8 *Love suffers long and is kind; love does not envy; love does not parade itself, is not puffed up; does not behave rudely, does not seek its own, is not provoked, thinks no evil; does not rejoice in iniquity, but rejoices in truth; bears all things, believes all things, hopes all things, endures all things. Love never fails...*

In this exercise, I want you to suppose you have only one day to live, now write a letter to your wife, telling her why you love her, and what you believe you would want her to know, and what you would do in your remaining hours with her and family. As I have mentioned earlier you share a special intimacy with your wife and there is no room for self pride, so I want you to just pour your heart out to her.

His Answers Cont.

<u>Her Answers</u>

I want you to suppose you have only one day to live, now write a letter to your husband, telling him why you love him, and what you believe you would want him to know, and what you would do in your remaining hours with him and family. As I have mentioned earlier you share a special intimacy with your husband and there is no room for self-pride, so I want you to just pour your heart out to him.

Her Answers Cont.

Conclusion: I wrote this book as a tribute to my beautiful wife and best friend, Linda, who will always hold a special place, deep in my heart. It has been a few years now since she went home to the Lord and she is still deeply loved and dearly missed by both family and friends. I have tried to share our belief that marriage is a life-long commitment between two people who love each other.

> Mark 10:6-9 *But from the beginning of the creation, God made them male and female. For this reason a man shall leave his father and mother and be joined to his wife, and the two shall become one flesh; so then they are no longer two, but one flesh. Therefore what God has joined, let no man separate.*

As I have said, our marriage wasn't perfect and I don't believe that any are, but we persevered and the longer we were together, the better it all seemed to get. My thoughts and prayers are that if you are willing to work hard at it, and make no mistake, there will be sacrifices, hard times and some may seem unbelievably tough, but if you stick it out and work at it, you will also see how wonderful it can be.

Remember that marriage is not a "give all or take all" arrangement, but a bit of both from each of you. We totally believed in the following verse:

> 1 Corinthians 7:10-11, *"Now to the married I command, yet not I but the Lord: **A wife is not to depart from her husband**.*

*But even if she does depart, let her husband remain unmarried or be reconciled to her husband. **And a husband is not to divorce his wife".***

If there are issues between the two of you that need the help of a trained individual, then don't put it off any longer, the Lord commands us to "humble ourselves", go and talk to your pastor, minister or a marriage counselor. Don't give up on your commitment.

Thank you and may God bless and keep the both of you together.

Printed in the United States
121410LV00003B/1-207/P

9 781606 473993